Imagine Sisyphus Happy

Imagine Sisyphus Happy

Poems by

R.G. Evans

Cover design by Shay Culligan
Cover art by Paul Dancik

ISBN: 978-1-952326-60-8

Kelsay Books
502 South 1040 East, A-119
American Fork, Utah, 84003

Acknowledgments

Painted Bride Quarterly: "Origin Story"

San Diego Poetry Annual: "Moon at Day"

Tiferet (Winner: 2017 Poetry Writing Prize): "Good Grief"

Backlash (U.K.): "The One-Armed Gravedigger," "Wallace Stevens Speaks to Me in Dreams"

IthacaLit: "Light Alone"

SurVision (Ireland): "Every Story Is a Ghost Story," "Yellow Poem, Blue Poem, Red Poem," "Deal," "All Newborn Gods"

Schuylkill Valley Journal: "Americana," "Apology to Time"

Paterson Literary Review: "The Year in Goodbyes," "Chronology"

The Harpoon Review: "Instead of Smiling"

Rose Red Review: "Snake Garden," "My Father Is a Cypress"

The Good Men Project: "Not Our Cat, Not Our Zucchini"

Philadelphia Stories: "Imagine Sisyphus Happy"

Nuclear Impact (Anthology): "Fallout"

Rattle: "Almost Holy"

Molecule: "Epigraph"

Lips: "Hangover Aubade"

The Blue Nib: "The Fantastic End of America"

Contents

I

Moon at Day

Pulling down the rotten boards
of a swing set no longer loved,
I feel you up there over my shoulder.
I built these swings myself
a dozen years ago. The tilt,
the lurch, my work for sure.
Now I pull it down and you pull too,
eye that couldn't wait for the night.
The tide in me rises to think
of those unborn children
who might have made me keep
these posts from falling apart.
A little paint. A little patch.
Maybe you're one of them,
looking down on me now
as I go about my best work:
destruction. Only one of you there,
precocious, ignoring bedtime.
Where's the other?
Maybe Halley's Comet, silver sibling,
running wild across the heavens,
not to return till I'm most surely gone.
These boards are full of rusty nails.
My knees creak like the gallows.
My daughter is sealed away in her room
writing stories that don't include me.
Only you can see me wipe my eyes
that burn in the lowering sun.
Only you have the grace to linger
as sky gives way to sky, empty blue
to a black freckled with impossible light.

Good Grief

At the high school's winter concert,
the frowning old man across the aisle
starts bopping his head and smiles
when the band begins to play
A Charlie Brown Christmas.
Sweet. A little miracle. But then
I see he's not that old—my age,
I'd say—and my own foot is tapping, too.
The band hits the jazzy little piano riff
and my chest opens like a silver dish,
a magician producing a dove. Ta-DA!
It flaps white wings and I'm back
belly-down on the ratty brown carpet
in my parents' living room.
Our first color TV has only three channels
and on one of them, that round-headed
sad sack is mourning his pathetic tree.
Good grief. Behind me sit my parents.
I feel them more than see them. They are alive
and I am young, so many years to go
before time strips all greenery from our tree.
Linus with his blanket. Schroeder's piano.
Lucy selling therapy at five cents a pop.
The frowning man with a smile on his face
closes his eyes and I know
he's in his own childhood's house.
It's good, this grief, these wings
lifting us both toward the light.
Good grief, bless old men
as they wander cartoon pasts
on the melodies of beautiful children.

Grief, be good to young musicians
when so many years transpose their keys to minor.
Let a white dove light in the saddest of trees.
Let us always remember this song.

Elegy Flowers

This winter, the elegy flowers bloom
like luminaria along the cemetery path.
We circle outward like pilgrims
traveling a labyrinth, flanked by markers
the stonecutters made, our sentries.
Fewer women are here than before.
The elegy flowers miss their tears
but are nearly drowned by our own.
Here in this halting winter light,
stopping is the only way to begin.
Lay your hands upon these stones
and make the only prophecy
you know will come true.
When you lift your hands again,
the stone's white coldness
will remain on your palms.
Press one against your brow,
the other to your lips.
Your petals are lovely as snow,
their whiteness proof
that you have lingered in the cold.

The One-Armed Gravedigger

never blames his tools

never leans on his shovel, waiting

understands the importance of time, yours and his

knows good work can't be rushed

always gets to work early, sometimes before anyone has even died

cuts the edges of earth straight from right to left

waits twice as long as he needs to after everyone has gone

shovels the earth back in reverently before tamping it down

feels self-conscious praying, but always says a prayer, after

can bend an elbow with the best when he knows he won't be
    needed

can count the times he wasn't needed on the fingers of one hand

For Fear of What the Neighbors Will Say

You aren't the only one
who has that notion,
that thought that crosses
your mind a minimum of
once a day. No princely
counter arguments,
just slings and arrows
that graze your flesh
and make you cry
enough. Acute mortality
is a bummer. Just ask
the Sextons down the road
(though in truth there aren't
nearly as many Sextons now
as there were just a while ago).
You might look into your mirror
one night and find that it's
a window and you, a voyeur.
Or you might find your seat
on a midnight train with a ticket
you thought was yours alone.
A tap on your shoulder,
and there's dear old Mrs.
Woolf from across the way.
You face the darkened window
where both of you shine palely
in the glass. At least the train
keeps moving. At least you're
going somewhere.

Like as Not

Mother has died
like a storm on a barren planet,
thunder fading into echoes
over crags and into canyons.

Mother has died
like a moth inside a window screen,
insignificant wings
creating no chaos but their own.

Mother has died
like an ibex on the savannah,
fleet of foot, the fastest beast alive
until she wasn't.

Mother has died
like God in the minds of moderns.
Talk to her every day—
the only response is silence.

Mother has died
like the refrain of a song.
Mother has died,
everybody sing along.

Light Alone

My never-babies, One and Two,
I'm glad you never came,
glad you never shared this house
with bottles and a passed-out man,
never had to see your living sister
go to him as a toddler
in his heap upon the floor
and snuggle as if he were aware
of her need and her love.
As if he were aware.
We planted flowering cherries for you,
but that's not where I see you
when I say the conjuring words.
I see you both in jars—not in some
murky, sideshow fluid
like the alcohol he keeps you in
next to the jar where he keeps himself—
I see you both in jars of light,
preserved in light alone
so you may see the way you nearly came.

My Daughter Turns Three Again

She whispers *It's today!* and she might be right.
She knows my memory is full of holes—
this birthday reminder a gift she gives me
again and again, Sometimes it's spring
and she is dewy April, eyes the blue of
rain-cleared skies. Sometimes in leafsmoke
autumn, she is Amber, giggling at the nights
that come too soon. Her favorite years
are those with more than one birthday.
She lets me know *It's today!* each time.
It might as well be every day, elusive
as icing on a cake that's never baked.
Not a celebration but a wish left unfulfilled.
It's today! soon turns to *Why was I never born?*
I can't answer with a song, a card, or an X
on a calendar square. Can't even promise
I'll be here for the next one. All I can do
is remember, though my memory's full of holes.
And my breath. My heart. My love.

Every Story Is a Ghost Story

The heart brims full with
libraries of the dead,
Alexandrias that never run out
of flames. For one tale
we leave out whiskey and blood-
red beef. For another the tribute
is rice and the Sunday comics.
A hundred dead monkeys hammer
a hundred dead keyboards.
One begins as a self-help book
and ends as an amnesiac's memoir.
Let the digitizing begin:
the world's run out of pulp
and circumstance demands a reckoning.
Alas, the book club is putting on weight:
here we are again and just last week,
tea and cakes.

Americana

Sometimes I see eagles.
A bald taking flight from
the middle of the road.
A golden perched
on the carcass of a deer.
Mostly, I see vultures
wheeling overhead on thermals.
Heads featherless to cleanly
burrow into viscera.
Their only natural means of defense,
projectile vomiting. When it's hot,
they piss on themselves to keep cool
and spread their wings as if they belonged
on the back of some dark doubloon.
They'll flock in a single tree
and return there like fruit each year.
Down the road they perch
on the First Presbyterian steeple
like metaphors. Every time
I see one fly, I think *eagle*
and am disappointed.
Every time they see me pass,
they're disappointed but think
We'll wait.

The Plague

Mostly now we stay inside,
forgetting: our mother's eyes,
the color of our first pet's fur.

Today is here. We can touch it.
Smell it. Taste it on our tongues.
But yesterday feels as if its edge

is frayed, its colors shrinking
inward like a flower unblooming.
Beyond that, gray and white

dance like fugitives tranquilized
and chained. No one noticed
till somebody died.

When we looked in the shoebox
handed down by our parents,
instead of the afterlife, nothing.

On the news they called it war—
chemical, cyber, jihad—
till all the TVs drifted

into snow. There's only us
between these walls now
in what might as well be

the dark. In one hand,
I hold an empty frame,
filling its borders

from memory. In the other,
I hold another's hand. Yours?

All Lie Down

The unweaving starts in September.
Fingers cunning as Penelope's
unravel one thin thread at a time.

First, a chill wind blows, just a breath
to cut through summer's final heat.
This is the month I was born.

Trees redden one leaf at a time.
This is the month my mother died.
In the fields, the farmer cuts the corn.

This is the month my father died.
Soon the time turns Pagan
and frost's first fingers clasp in prayer.

The veil grows thin. No need
for shears to cut the final thread.
Once the last stitch is loosed,

I press my lips to my suitor's mouth.
This is the month we all lie down.

Momentary

The cut dry hay of August,
its scent a little like decay,
deranges time and I am a child
at the carnival by the train tracks.
Straw spread over paths of mud.
Bamboo canes. Hawaiian leis.
Chinese finger traps. A carousel
in the rain. *Boo-boo,* my mother calls,
don't wander off too far,
but when I turn there's only open fields,
the tractor and two men gone, bales
the size of caskets on their sides.

On Seeing a Facebook Notification That Today Is the Birthday of a Friend Who Died Last Week

In memory of Jim Breech

It startles the heart,
like icy water startles the skin,
into remembering that in this world
we are always between angels.
So many times this week
your face popped up on this screen
in grief and shock and suddenness
that when I see you now
with the gentle reminder
that today is your birthday,
that you'd be sixty-six,
that I should write something to you,
for a moment there is no air.
What would I say to you now?
How's the electronic afterlife?
What stopped your athlete's heart?
Hurray!—you're sixty-five forever?
I close my laptop just so I can breathe
in a room without an angel—
and my phone chirps, the way they do
alerting me of the unbearable heaviness
of unexpected wings.

Lucky

Luck is one breath in and one breath out.
It's the blood pressure running high or low
but still running.
Luck is the way the food stays down
for the first time in over a week.
Ask around. You'll find what feels lucky to others:
>—*It's when my father finally left my addict mom*
>*even though we sleep now on our cousin's floor*
>—*It's a day when the pain in my uterus*
>*isn't bad enough to make me scream*
>—*It's the voice of God that found me*
>*after my husband found an HIV-infected whore*
>—*It's the deadline that keeps my mind off*
>*the lump still growing in my breast*
>—*It's finding out the police are here*
>*for my father, not for me*

Lucky the little dog barks every time the front step creaks.
Lucky the razor stays locked up in its case.
Lucky the hand is no longer a fist.
If you want to feel lucky, take a look at a stone.
If your name isn't carved there, it's your lucky day.

The Ice Cream Man

The hands that reached out
from the Mister Softee truck
always seemed hot when he handed us
the already dripping sweetness.
Share, he'd always say in a frozen voice.

Someone or something reminded me
lately of the sound of his chimes,
the way they always seemed to
climb in pitch on the air as he approached
then grow heavy as a dirge as he left us there behind.

What bitter roads he'd driven,
thankless streets, shuttered houses,
until he stopped in front of ours,
dark as the rest for all we knew,
our hungry backs turned upon our lives.

Did any other lips but mine
ever plunge into the pillar of cream
that oozed down over my wrist?
How do you share what can't be shared?
What use is memory

meant for hot hands, blue music
that can't carry its tune,
a single commandment uttered,
as hard to bear as the stone
whereon its word was never carved?

Puss Irvin

—for my father

We all knew she was a witch.
We'd see her through the windows
of her broken house on Tenth Street
swaying in her near-dark parlor,
pulling night down over the town.
We'd dare each other to touch the stone
on the edge of her front yard,
so black and full of stars
it must have come from outer space.
And we knew a hex sign when we saw one:
like the flag that appeared one day
in her window, edged in blood red
with one blue star—maybe the star
she called that black rock down from.

At the Rialto matinee, we'd watched
The Wizard of Oz a dozen times,
nodding sagely as only stupid boys can do
whenever Dorothy melted the witch.
Now, with the men in town gone to war,
we knew what we had to do.

We raided Tindall's henhouse
and fired egg after egg at Puss's house,
coating windows and walls,
blurring that hex sign in the window—
until Puss burst through the door
and we ran faster than black magic.

We stayed away till Halloween,
till the pull of mischief grew too strong.
More eggs, more boys this time—
but when we got to Puss's house,

we saw some alchemy had changed
that blue hex star to gold.
Before we threw a single egg,
the door opened and Puss emerged.
She pointed at us then clasped her hands
as if to pray, crying *Why?*

Strong alchemy:
blue into gold, witch into woman,
mischief into guilt and shame.
We left the eggs there in the yard
by the great black stone
whose darkness, now it seemed,
could only have come from Earth.

II

The Year in Goodbyes

Poor Father Time. Every year kicks his ass.
He comes in fresh with his little sash
like a Best Baby Contest winner,
but leaves broken and bearded,
turning his hunched back
on the babe sent in to take his place.
That's all we ever see.
The coming. The going.
The geezer and the babe.
What of the rest of the year?
The toddler in February,
playing catch with Cupid's darts.
The "whining schoolboy" of March,
praying the longest month will end.
The horny lad of spring,
flirting with April and May.
But he's more than just the calendar.
Like us, all his lives are different.
He can feel a month's headlines
in his arthritic knees.
Global news gives him lumbago.
Oh, and what some elections
do to his hemorrhoids.
When the whole thing winds down—
top 10 lists, the year in review and in goodbyes—
he looks back as well at that apple-cheeked cherub
born in ignorance and hope, still
able to dream without meds.
There's a knock at Father's door.

On the other side, the new babe is waiting.
Some tongues, he knows,
have the same word for *hello* and *goodbye*.
How easily, he thinks, that sash
could become a garotte.
He and the innocent exchange a glance,
one of them suddenly lost in translation.

Instead of Smiling

On the obituary page,
the dead are always smiling,
as if watching the birdy
when they were alive
prepared them for
the secret birds of paradise.
We learn when young
to smile for cameras
or the toys that dip
and dangle behind them.
But why not scowl
or cower pop-eyed,
weep instead of grinning,
preserve the whole
history of our faces
while we still suffer time?
We owe it to the frowning future
to leave dead headshots
of truth. The shutterbugs
should start us young,
forego the birdies
and dangle strangled cats,
see what words choke out
instead of *cheese.*

Origin Story

On the day they gave out superpowers,
I said I wanted to be invincible.
The Creator, old and feeble even then,
Blinked and squinted. I knew he didn't hear.
And just like that, I became invisible.
Some around me dashed away at super speed,
Some took flight, burning in the sky like meteors,
but there I stood. Not that anybody noticed.
Mortal, invisible, alone. Bullets could riddle me
and no one would even see my blood.
A speeding train might run me down—
the engineer would only feel a bump.
I asked the Creator what I was supposed to do.
He cocked his head like a curious dog
and walked away. That's my origin story,
how I became the incredible not-there man,
king of entrances and exits, master of being ignored.
I let my hair grow shaggy—why should I care
about appearances? I stopped bathing
till I was just an odor passing through the world.
I sometimes saw crimes, but the criminals
didn't see me. Why should I get involved?
I gave up food and water and began to fade away,
though I'm the only one who knows,
not even you beside me now as I die,
living your life, thinking your thoughts,
effortlessly reflecting light.

Hero's Journey

Like the man arriving alone on the Haj
two cities over from Mecca,
this pilgrimage is to the wrong place.
The beloved author never lived
in the house you're taking selfies with.
Her house is up the hill and three blocks north.
Wander all you will, you'll never find the bones
of the great man you seek in this cemetery.
You passed his final place miles ago.
Still there's something to be said
about the journey itself—and what's said is
The journey of a thousand miles begins…
blah, blah, blah, something about the steppe.
And where is that, exactly? You never see it
on your map. Your compass rose is withered,
and the North Star points toward Ultima Thule.
But wasn't that a bad guy from *Star Trek,* or
Star Wars, or…whatever? It's like you
always say: *No matter where you go,*
where am I?

Snake Garden

—in memory of Russell Edson

A woman was sowing snakes in the garden.

"Don't be foolish," her husband told her. "It's too early to plant copperheads. You have to wait until the last frost is past."

The woman ignored his advice. "That's an old wives' tale," she said, sowing another row.

"You should know," he told her. "You're an old wife. But we shall see come the next frost."

The next night grew frigid, and when morning came, the woman awoke to find a fine blanket of ice silvering her garden.

"You see," her husband said. "You should have planted something heartier, like timber rattlers or cottonmouths."

"I will plant mambas in your work boots," she told him. "And coral snakes in your sock drawer."

"That's no way for a wife to talk," he said.

"I'm no wife," the woman said. "I'm a gardener—see?"

The man turned to find delicate vines covered with silver scales sprouting in the garden through the ice.

"You are a gardener!" he said.

"I am a wife," the woman said. "Now it's back to the snake store. Mind your boots and socks."

No Time to Wallow in the Mire

There's always time, babe—
or so I'd tell my ex-old lady,
claim Oscar Wilde said it first
but she'd say he said gutter
and that other part about
looking at the stars (some of us).
Sometimes I'd say William Blake—
hell, that's where Morrison got
The Doors (of perception)—
but she'd say no, say anyway
you really want to model yourself
on a dead fat man in a bathtub
and I'd say Little Feat and she'd say
nothing for a good long time.
I'd say into her silent time
see, right here's a bunch of time
to wallow in the mire, but she'd
turn up her nose (looking at the stars?)
and I'd be left to hum ole Ray
Manzarek's hypnotic solo,
popping beers till I was hypnotic, solo.
Be drunk, I'd say. Baudelaire, I'd say
but there was no one else left in the silence,
no one to care about my dead French
mire wallowers, no one but me,
hands empty, head full of lazy revolution,
the last martyred slave of time.

Not Our Cat, Not Our Zucchini

Family shorthand,
origin lost.
Not our cat.
Not our zucchini.
Automatic as *gesundheit,*
just as meaningless.
Secret language
of the blood-bound,
untranslatable.
To end a fight,
to pick a fight,
to raise a storm of laughter.
Not our cat.
Not our zucchini.
After a death, we hear it
in the voice of the departed
echoing into infinity,
just another yodel
down the Alps of evermore.
Moons will wheel
from New to Full.
Someone will trip,
Drop an egg or keys
or F-bomb.
Not our cat,
some cantor will chant.
Not our zucchini,
the faithful will respond,
and just like that
it will be true again:
We are all alive.

Just Like a Fool

This is the journey of a thousand
first steps. Did I leave the stove burning
with lost desire? Have I forgotten my keys
from Largo to Islamorada?
I was thrown out of the band called
Major Arcana for faking wisdom.
Just like a fool. Who questions his right
to dignity doesn't deserve life's
question marks. He should double down
as I have on the bitter exclamation points.
I crusaded for the conservation
of matter, but who has the energy anymore?
Still I will step into every day and strike
while the iron—which I may have left on—is hot.

Convenience

The last thing you expect to see at 7-
Eleven is a hearse. But there it was,
all shiny black and final. Some say heaven
is one long chill pill, high without the buzz.
It makes you think of things like that I guess
when Black Moriah pulls into your lot.
You sip your coffee, pretending no distress—
but *Why the hell's that here's* your only thought.
It's not for gas: there aren't any pumps.
The driver's staying put—and those in back?
No Slurpee in the world can make them jump—
eternal brain freeze in that Cadillac.
Like mystery itself, just like the grave,
it came, it went, it conquered through dismay.

Wallace Stevens Speaks to Me in Dreams
(Because He Doesn't Speak to Me
on the Page)

He and I are not one. He and I and black night are not one,
but his voice awakens within me as I dream, says

concupiscence and the lack of a good concordance
are not excuse enough, says

Anecdote of the Lazy Reading, says
Anecdote of the Internet-addled Mind, says

sing beyond the genius,
beyond the rage for order, says

have a mind of winter and let yourself be
haunted by white nightgowns, says

Anecdote of Resistance, says
Anecdote of the One Who's Lost His Way, says

I placed a jar in Tennessee and all you did
was lift it to your lips and drink, says

you will awaken and not know which to prefer:
the whistling or just after, says

all there is is just after just after
the finale of seem—and I know what he says

is true enough for dreams
if not for the mind who dreams them.

III

Imagine Sisyphus Happy

Does he whistle as he sweats and groans
the boulder up the mountain?
Does he ever think *At least I'm not at home*
where my daughter wants to die
trembling there at the summit
just before the rock rolls down?
As he follows it, his mind might wander
to the time his daughter screamed
Sixteen years in this goddamn house
with your failed marriage as my roommate!
What did she know about what god has damned?
Maybe he smokes, letting gravity do its job
one step at a time. Eternity is eternity after all,
no room here for a goldbricking soul.
If one can imagine Sisyphus happy,
it isn't hard to picture him grinding his smoke
beneath his toe, cracking his knuckles,
and glancing at Tantalus in his lake
beneath the trees, bending as the water recedes.
And yet, Sisyphus wonders,
was that a wink he saw from his damned neighbor
when the fruit pulled away out of reach?
At least the bastard's in the shade, he thinks
and shrugs his flesh into the stone.

The Pagan World

never lets us forget it's still here.
The temples all closed,
Pan frolics from minaret to steeple,
exchanging the song of his pipes
for the sound of wind across stones.
Apollo blazes, Artemis glows
brighter than ever in the newly detoxified air.
Zeus, nostalgic for the flood,
chuckles as if tickled by lightning
at empty gymnasiums and amphitheaters.
In the unfamiliar stillness, Ares waits. And plans.
Overworked in the underworld,
Hades wrings his hands
as if imitating the new arrivals
acting out washing their own.
And out on every deserted road,
Pandora shakes her nearly empty box,
rattling inside her one gift that remains.

God of Ghosts

Belief is the enemy of the god of ghosts.
He knows it's what created him, knows
too that many lose it early, between
their milk teeth and virginity.
What's the use of being a king
if even a rook is the pawn of doubt,
if the chess board looks deserted
to the eyes of the would-be haunted?
Death is the least of his misfortunes
when the other ghosts can see
right through him. Who can moan
the loudest? Who can chill a room
the coldest? Who can stop the breath
the quickest when a hand gropes
for the lights? But no hand comes
groping. That sound in the night
is merely snoring. Times are tough
on both sides of the veil. Sometimes
he can't even believe in himself.

All Newborn Gods

All newborn gods
are anonymous as birdsong.
They speak the same language
of need, dance the same mazurka
in cradle, crib, or creche.
All newborn gods bestow
blessings of shit and piss
unto a world that doesn't know
it needs changing as well.
The parents of all newborn gods
are as stunned as virgins
visited by angels screaming
hosannas in the middle of the night
while the unblessed world sanely sleeps.
All newborn gods
could eat the sun and moon,
the earth and all the sky,
would devour their own tails
if it weren't for the swaddling clothes.
Over the heads of all newborn gods,
stars cluster like berries. Pick one.
It's as good as any other:
the light where all begins.

Chronology

We are older than our scars.
            —*Richard Hugo*

All of us are twins,
born into the same litter
as our suffering.
And in our secret language,
the line is always open between us.
Some of us have outlived
our passions, outgrown our loves.
Estranged from gods
we never knew believed in us,
we mourn time's passing
as if it were our own.
Overhead, those still older siblings,
the sun and the moon,
rise and set, wax and wane
to remind us that for now
we are younger than our deaths
as we have always been
and always will be
so long as we breathe
and breathe again.

Stay

I once had a dog I loved
to beat with sticks, chains,
the backs of my bare hands.

He'd flatten his ears and yelp,
run away and stay away for days,
then come back, tail wagging.

I used to think God was a cur
with snarling, snapping jaws,
an appetite for my throat alone.

Now I know that I was right
to beat whatever dog I could
find, mine, yours, whosever.

Now I know that I'm that dog,
the wretched scent of home
irresistible.

Christ on the Cross

In the old church, Christ on the cross
was thin as a nail and beyond all suffering,
xylophone ribs, spine nearly visible
through the wasted muscles of his belly.
Then they tore the old church down
and built a new one, all glass and
angular wood. The New Age called
for a new Christ, still on the cross
but risen, guru's robes and Beatles beard,
arms forward and beckoning.
They saved the old Christ, though—
or maybe he just came back unbidden,
the way that Christs do—relegated
to the dark little side chapel, where,
if you wanted to pray to the god
of yesteryear and agony, he'd welcome you
with open—albeit broken—arms.

Fallout

Beside the crucifix in the Catholic school lunchroom
hung a black and yellow fallout shelter sign.
We'd cross ourselves for Grace, but instead of praying

I'd think of fallout, imagine it as snow-like flakes,
gray and silent, floating down to cover and burn
everything they touched. Born too late for air raid drills,

we had no rituals to teach us how to fear the atom
like the ones that showed us how to fear our Lord.
Nuns taught us geometry and about the triune God,

but I studied the yellow trinity of triangles
inside that priest-black circle. One for the Father,
one for the Son, and one for the Holy Ghost

who moved across creation as a dove, a breath—
or as tongues of flame that descended upon the Apostles
at Pentecost. Christ's isosceles wounds watched over us

as we ate lunch amid the mysteries of our faith,
sheltered from any fire that might fall out of the sky.

Prayer

Praise the quilt the mother handed down.
Her spirit holds each hand-stitched square together.

Praise the crust of bread that isn't enough today.
It may be more than you will have tomorrow.

Praise the restless the reckless the wild.
Teach the fearful and timid to sing their songs.

Praise the achievement of the lilac opening fragrant
in the spring. Praise the bee who shares the flower's praise.

Praise the avant-garde of madness. They see
truths none of us has yet to find—but someday will.

Praise the dervish and the inanimate too. Who's to say
which is holier, the one in motion or the one who is still?

Praise the emptiness within that calls us forth to praise.
It may be all we have and may be, praise be, enough.

The End of Worship

We who can't endure
the tiny truth of our own
mortality presume to believe
that God is dead.
Something set the stars alight.
Nothing yet has snuffed them
one by one, like an acolyte
dowsing candles at the end of worship.
One might blame the artists,
the writers of the word who,
unable to see beyond their own images,
grafted wings and halos
onto the bodies of men.
Likely the mad chant
a more boundless truth.
Press an ear to their silently
ranting lips, and you may hear
syllables that burn like fueled stars,
an indecipherable prayer, almost saying,
Take these wings, this fire from my head.
Let me live in the dust
the blinded way that others do.

IV

At the Border of the Day

We are all refugees at the border of the day.
Night enveloped us in its cloaky arms
whispering lies of safe haven, whispering
these blankets are magic blankets,
nothing can harm you here.
But the sun comes up and we have to show our papers,
wear neutral faces through the inspection,
pretend we speak the lingua franca of existence
and pass among others as if we're one of them.
Every greeting is a test of our training,
every casual exchange a chance to betray ourselves.
We wear our mask of kinship,
our blank kabuki false face, and pray
the day accelerates, time-lapses us to safety
so we can slip unnoticed again into
dreams we pray are humble,
that we may awaken to a blank sunrise
that will only show our lack of self,
that will let us rise and step into
our midnight minds again.

Beauty

isn't
the rose

it's
the thorn

its kiss
upon

the
fingertip

the gift
of one red

drop
that's

traveled
through

the
heart

Enemies of Time

We are all enemies of time,
the way we rise again each day
like suns or moons or stars
who don't know their fire's burning out.
We invented time like Frankenstein,
no regard for our creation or what
the hands of clocks might do to us
if they could reach our mortal necks.
Every pain, every scar, every weakness
is a scream that we are still here,
that the great river raging around us
hasn't yet pulled us from this rock,
that we stand against the tide,
the greedy moon's pull, the darkness
that knows we are bound for it soon.
Our hands are the hands of a child
clutching a much larger hand,
pretending we are safe, we are eternal.
In imagination we are everlasting
and time loathes a dreamer and the dream.
It waits for us to wake—
all time knows how to do—
but the night is long and our sleep as sound
as mortar fire keeping the enemy at bay.

Perchance to Dream

The little sorrows of the bed
make me hesitate at night,
a pause, a breath before my body
conforms to its sleeping self
and sinks under the smooth, dark wave
of helplessness. Inside my dream
I can hide nowhere. The barbed wire edges
of sleep herd me into empty rooms,
bare shelves proof that
all the dream books disappear.
Here, I am a beggar without hands enough
to find them empty, my tear-erased face
only a placeholder between my collar
and my hood. I've had a lover here—
I can smell her on the wind—but
she lives beyond the place
where water holds no shape.
She could not still my night-trapped heart.
The narrative changes, and from another world,
a man's voice yelling *Sir!* into my ear
that fills like a cup of cotton seeds and spills me
into the bright choking hands of dawn.

Prophecy

A star streaks over the countryside.
A grandmother shoos crows
with a broom. Little ripples
like the famous butterfly
whose wings stir up a hurricane.
Auspices are everywhere.
The tread of a girl's shoe
preserved in the mud of time.
The cave wall that crumbles
and gives the world the Taung child.
Not all lives involve momentous
signs—flack that brings the plane down
but spares the pilot's life.
We all are sedimentary,
the stairsteps of every yesterday
leading up to ourselves of today.
Think of the time-lapse tide
embracing a pier. We are that tide
and we are the pier. We are
the very passing of time
that brings about the embrace.
Our father the prophet.
Our mother the prophecy.
Yesterday knew that we would all come true.

No Wonder

The desk clerk's accent
assured me that I was
in the wrong place.
I only stay where
I'm not wanted. Take home,
for instance, where there's
a maximum five years'
stay and I'm going on
twenty. No wonder
the clerk gave me a key
only to the beach.
No wonder no turn
down service. No wonder
at the water's edge
all I have is
tern, tern, tern.

How to Keep Warm

Play with fire.
Burn down a house
no matter whose.
Have a meltdown.
Sing a torch song.
Carry a torch
for someone.
Fall into a ring of fire.
Fan the flames.
Kindle an old flame.
Press the flesh.
Do a slow burn.
Burn bridges.
Rub together
sticks and stones.
Strike sparks.
Strike while the iron's hot.
Fly too close to the sun.
Journey to the underworld.
Be a firewalker.
Drink firewater.
Catch fireflies.
Get fired up.
Add fuel to the fire.
Open fire.
Get caught in a crossfire.
Burn a cross.
Burn out.
Run.

Adagio

There is another voice
like a single, strangled violin string
that keeps the world aloft,

all its stony gravity
rising, falling, forgotten.

Wordless, tuneless, barely bold enough
to be called music, it's lost
inside the great roar of machines,

of wings, of the very atoms
that make up the blood.

Sometimes the sound of waking,
sometimes that of the napping eye.
Unheard, it beckons, lips tremble.

No one dares applaud before the movement's end.
Nor here, it seems, in the aftersilence.

Apology to Time

We who have cursed you
for leaving us too soon and for
congealing like marrow around us,
we who see that you get wasted,
a pledge allowed neither sleep nor sobriety,
we who tried to conquer you
with sand and shadows,
gears and cogs,
microchips and diodes,
we who mark you, waste you,
limit you and beat you,
use your signatures as our own,
we who end up doing you because
we've already done something worse,
we who rest when you are out
and expire when you are up
apologize for killing you when young
and later for trying to turn back your hands
when all you wanted to do was fly.

V

Almost Holy

My niece is addicting
mice to cocaine.

The cause is science,
the university is Temple

so it's almost holy.
Poor little buggers.

Their tickers get to ticking,
and pretty soon they dream

that they are rats,
that they can fly,

that they are rats
with wings, pigeons

soaring over mouse and rat,
the god of mice,

of rats, of birds. Until morning
when they'll believe

that they are dead.
Then the true god comes

in a cloud-like lab coat,
the resurrection and the life.

I used to dream
I was a mouse,

but I am only a flea
upon a mouse's back.

But sometimes . . . sometimes
the blood is so sweet

I feel I'm the uncle of light riding
bareback and holy through the temple.

Yellow Poem, Blue Poem, Red Poem

Yellow poem says it's sorry
that everything passes away.
Sunset. Oak leaves in fall—
you know, the things poets say
when they mean they are afraid.
Yellow poem says go on,
be afraid. Be yellow.
If you never write a poem again,
at least you'll still have fear.

Blue poem says come on and
have a drink. It knows twelve bars
where you can sink good and deep
down in the blue. It says
the sky ain't cryin', baby.
That's just words to take the place
of a scream that would come out blue.
Blue poem says now drink. Now smoke.
Come be the whole blue goddam sky.

Red poem don't say nothing.
Red poem is a rope with one knot
in your chest, one knot in your throat,
one knot right between your eyes.
Red poem knows you know
it's the one true poem.
It's in your blood. It's in your eyes.
It's the color your words make
when you ain't got time
for no more yellow or blue.
Red poem's the one with teeth.
Red poem's got you by the balls.

My Father Is a Cypress

His bayou is my bayou, his knees my knees,
pushing himself up within me toward the sky
neither of us will reach. Angerwood
twists upward, unable to hold its needles
like conifers without rage. How can I tell
his cinnamon from my gold
when our silences sound identical?
How can the living contain the dead
when the dead were here first?
My father is not a cypress. I am not a tree,
but I contain him like a seed within a cone.
We stand knee-deep in tea-colored water,
draw it into ourselves through roots gone bad,
father and son, deciduous and drowning.

My Finally Upright Life

When I was upside down,
head on the curb,
feet pointed in prayer toward heaven,
I believed that birds were fish
swimming in the waterless air.
You're not like us,
the right-side uppers said,
their grins like frowns
from where I stood.
Cardinals like Betas
hurled their bodies into glass.
You won't get very far in life like that,
said the voices attached to the feet
passing by my head.
Goldfinches, goldfish.
Everything was golden.
Then, out of a pocket—
one of mine? one of theirs?—
a key dropped and clattered by my head.
When I reached for it, I reached down.
When I picked, I picked it up.
And suddenly it was the key
to my finally upright life.
Eye-to-eye with others at last,
I was like all the rest,
and the starfish all were starlings,
common, bland, everywhere.

Love Poem

I'll put on my burlap mask, the one
with the unbuttoned eyes
and zigzag stitch for a smile.

You shimmy into the next ten years
like a satiny slip of rainwater
falling softly from cloudless skies.

The band will play the Too Late Tango.
Under candy-colored lights,
we'll stalk each other like prey.

This must be what they mean
when they say *restraining order,*
this fatal hook and eye fastness.

We'll be the quick till we'll be the dead,
spinning, agitated, and clean
beyond all cleanliness.

Some say, *We know trauma
when we see it.* But we're deaf
and laughing like Parisian sirens

on a blood-red ambulance or two.

Deal

A deck of cards with unfamiliar suits tempts me
into gambling with a stake that I don't have.
Across the table, a bust of Nero
imagines itself with arms, what a winning hand it could hold.
Floorboards creak in the empty room upstairs,
and Nero and I look for a clock that doesn't exist,
no way to tell the hour when the birds all disappeared,
vacant trees testaments to their passing.
I look at my cards—the twelve of hats,
the murder of crows, the motherless son,
the question mark of suicide, the dunce of mirrors.
Nero has played a rainbow flush and I see that I am bust.
He gives an armless shrug, says *How am I to fiddle now?*
a question better than my answer,
My god has stopped working.

Epigraph

A paper bird in a fire tree
spread its wings and burned for me.
The sky was flame, the sun was coal,
the bird that burned had been my soul.
And I below in ghostless surprise
stood in air that crystallized
to bars, a prison for the dead
in a world forever burning red.

Hangover Aubade

I've swallowed the rising sun.
In my chest, behind my eyes,
it is pleading for the East.
My blood hangs loose in the sky.
Red bunting. Dread holiday.
I've traded places with the day
and the calendar cries foul.
I teach birds the secret language
of pain so they will know it
when next it pierces their breasts.
I spread a bilious dew in my wake
and wake to what feels like my wake.
I long to be a pantoum,
an abecedarian mystery,
the mystic repetition of a villanelle,
but I am fit only for dawn,
the edge of Earth scraping me
into being. A song best suited
for this one light, this one breath,
and (dear god) another.

"Education Is Not Preparation for Life; Education Is Life Itself."

—John Dewey

Picture a small-town library,
its creaky floors and limited
stacks. See in your mind's eye
a certain shelf of books,
Dewey's 100 for philosophy,
say, or maybe 800, literature
and rhetoric. Each spine
apparently unique. You've seen
libraries on TV, enough to emulate
what patrons do: you haul
an armload of books to an empty
table, adjust your glasses
(bought at Walgreens just for
the occasion) and start cracking
open covers. Strange that you
would find an epigraph in every book
and every one the same: "He will
rise from the dead and become
our friend." Oh dear, oh dear,
you think, mentally shushing yourself
as you eye the clock's hour hand.
You have a deadline to meet
and this will never do.

The Soy's Long Dream

Tonight is the last of the soy's long dream.
When it first went to sleep it was green as a bottle,
its leaves barely whispered in the wind.
Stretched over enough acres that it knew only
its own dominion, each plant could read
the flickering shadows that grew in all the others'
chlorophyll minds. Little by little it stiffened
and grew brown, the sounds of its sleeping
a rattle as dry as an ancient child's toy.
The soy doesn't know it's dreaming,
won't remember any of its collective dreams
in the morning when the reaper comes
and swings his wake-up call from the hip.
The harvester will raise it up, and the soy
may feel the silvery weight of the Hunter's Moon
upon its leaves, stems, and beans.
Or perhaps it never felt at all,
just moved when the wind moved it,
bent like the burdened in the rain,
while we pretended that it could dream,
that we could dream, that dreams
were what made us both alive.

"The Fantastic End of America"

—Jack Kerouac

First the bang. Then the whimper. Now this.
Our Lady of the Highways hitching a ride west
where even she believes she'll find the dream.

She ends up hoofing it, skulls like globes underfoot,
indigenous stepping stones across rivers
and arroyos, deserts and grassland plains.

All the ghosts along the way. The Pioneer Spirit
weeping on the edge of the trail. The Angel Moroni
climbing his own golden spires, like Kong winged but doomed.

Manifest Destiny itself barely recognizable
among the fast food chain cholesterol plants.
Progress may have stalled, but Our Lady keeps on

truckin', pedal to the metal, balling the jack,
following the sun as it falls out of the sky
somewhere in the Pacific, gentle waves lapping

the Nevada shoreline. Our Lady hikes up her skirt
and cools her aching dogs in the breakers.
It's there she sees it, washed up on the sand

like Charlton Heston's fever dream, the sign
edited by entropy like everything else:
HO LYWOOD.

About the Author

R.G. Evans is the author of two previous poetry collections, *Overtipping the Ferryman* and *The Holy Both.* His album of original songs, *Sweet Old Life,* is available on most music streaming services. Website: www.rgevanswriter.com.